Poets & Allies for Resistance 2015 Anthology

Copyright © 2016 Khadija Anderson
ISBN: 978-0-9912975-6-6
Published by Jamii Publishing
San Bernardino, CA
www.JamiiPublishing.com

All rights reserved. No part of this book may be reproduced, stored in a retrieval system, or transmitted in any form or by any means--- electronic, mechanical, digital, photocopy, recording, or any other--- except for brief quotations in printed reviews, without the prior permission of the publisher.

Poets & Allies for Resistance
2015 Anthology

Poets & Allies for Resistance is a monthly literary series featuring two writers of color and an open mic that focuses on social justice issues. The series was formed in response to and support of the Black Lives Matter movement and had it's first reading in December 2014 in Pasadena, CA.

Table of Contents

Ashaki Jackson — 1
Standard American Similes with Interchangeable Blacks — 1
The body of an American paratrooper — 2

Conney Williams — 3
equal protection — 3
a palestinian father's prayer — 5

Nikki Blak — 6
Black Lives — 6
Pathology — 8

Tommy Domino — 11
For Coconut — 11

AKoldPiece — 13
Haiku — 13

Pam Ward — 15
Breast Milk — 15
Panther Mothers — 17

Jawanza Dumisani — 18
Nightmare — 18
The Watch — 20

Derek Brown   *23*
Free-dumb!   23
Slaughterhouse   25

Kiyatana Sapp   *26*
Hoodwinked   26

Jennifer Thompson   *29*
Mother   29

Doug Kearney   *32*
Alameda Street   32
Tar   34

C. Imani Williams   *35*
Your Truth Matters: Live to Love,
   Release The Rest   35
YOU HAVE THE RIGHT NOT
 TO REMAIN SILENT   36

Biographies   *39*

Poets & Allies for Resistance
2015 Anthology

Ashaki Jackson

Standard American Similes with Interchangeable Blacks

The night is as black as skin   It falls slowly
   publicly like an {Eric}

Night hushes like a {Jordan}

Sky creeps like a Black body's blood   Sleepless
birds enforce curfew

The people are as broken and exposed as {Emmett}
Aren't we?

Time drags like {James}   Look how
the {Otis} levitates full-faced and pale among the black
walnut trees

Stars surround as quickly as officers   *Again* night is dark
like Mother's throat

Mother's cry is black with grief
                                        We have
moved into metaphor

*Previously published in: pluck! The Journal of Affrilachian Arts & Culture

The body of an American paratrooper killed in action in the jungle near Cambodian border is raised up to an evacuation helicopter (Henri Huet, 1966)

This body:
        a question and broken
        compass   North-pointing or ascending
        and bruised like a savior

I mean the body is dead

        Fully-clothed and suspended in a truth-
        ful place

When I say truthful   I mean honest
as skin   {A loose
tongue}   I'm saying
"obvious"   The body hides
nothing but prayer and low tide

retreating all
its breathless melody   Now: stiff
   slow in its arch   I swear he is a black-
necked stork cascading

So sure   his mother will open
her wide-mouthed wail   jowls brimming
with iridescent plumage   Her body too

passing through
surrender

*Previously published in: Rkvry Quarterly Literary Journal

Conney Williams

equal protection

y'all think Betsy
sewed black yarn into
thirteen stars and stripes
think, she use a thimble
to stitch magic
around its borders
that flag don't protect
some folk from the tempest
like it was s'posed to
I suspect it never waved
just hung
aloof in the distance
impotently upon a pole
allegiance for the blind
convince believers
it is refuge for ALL
most easily forget, Ol' Glory

                                        the banner of inequity

longer than Ol' Dixie ever was
but imma wear

it's intent anyhow
Lawd knows this rag
gots to be good for sumptin

a palestinian father's prayer

all of me is fragile, and
I have lost all hope
in this world
our blood
is a nickel a barrel
and we
have no oil
to barter for safety
death
moved into the apartment
next door
plans to move in
with me and my family
the air is shrapnel, and
my people desert
the world doesn't care
if we have a home
does anyone remember
we used to be a nation
all of me is fragile,
we have lost all hope
in this world

Nikki Blak

Black Lives

When God invented sound
We are what he intended
Us with our percussion footsteps
With our gleaming trumpets
With these lungs
With these mouths
My body, a clef
His nautilus ears
A many chambered
Masterpiece
And all the World
Altered, added, suspended

We were born knowing how
To prism these chords
Marry triad to rustling wind
Weave between
These trees, standing
Tambourine
The leaves, changing
To know the difference
To modify the time

To open the corridors
Of our throats
Forever and ever
And never have to sleep
Or wonder

We are unrelenting
8 count enough to fill a glass
Thunder enough to break it's back
Hands enough to carry it
Mend
Construct
Destroy again

We, symphony
Of hearts
Bleed riffs
Like the ancients
And our mothers' mothers
Their eyes, notation
Captured in
Collective memory
Like rainwater
Like morning
Like the tingle
Of sunlight
Coloring us green
Growing us big

Tuning our
Guitar string veins
Vibrating our bones
Puzzling us into
Gifts shaped
Like children

Pathology

We never told you
How we opened our arms
And enveloped an entire city
Made the skyscrapers kneel
And how their architectural angles
And tinted glass open mouth
Kissed us back like savages
Thirsty for our blood
Drank us to ash
We never told you how
We forgave it anyway
We stayed with our necks to it
Gave it soft bellies to part
Into a sea red with human
Our chests, without armor
Ran our tongues along it's cables
Hooked our claws to its bones
And beat a lullaby into it's palm
Constant and perfect
As a blueprint

We never told you
How we got here
Perched on top
Of this charred skeleton
A memory of a bridge
Its ruins, still exhaling smoke
into the atmosphere
Its spirit, ripe with indecision
Just as willing to haunt as it is
To lie down forever
Our eyes, still lit torches

So many and unblinking
The sky went blind

We never told you
About the scrape
Of hips against metal
And the light show
Of angry sparks
It creates

We never told you how
We had to remind ourselves
That we were still alive
How we had to
Jump start these hearts
Several times
And even then,
How the engine died
On the deserted road
How we lost count
Of the unmarked graves
How we had to ride the train
And the unforgivable things we did
To pay for the ticket

We never told you
How we found enough hands
To untie ourselves
How we traded limbs
For freedom
How we stained our lips
This particular shade
Of wrath

It is a bad story
Your tornado ears
Will swallow it
Will rearrange it
Vomit its entire distorted text
Into an empty field
Drop it onto some one's house
Destroy a life with it

Heavy as it is

It is because
We love, cannibalistic
Eat our prey alive, messy
It is because
We clean the bones
We cut new teeth
In rows
We sanctuary broken
So carnivorous we are
If you could only imagine
We would bite our own reflections
If the mirror
Would just let us in

Tommy Domino

For Coconut

G- Flat Baritone - tones - deep like
Like Muddy Waters; rolling stone, rolling stone, rolling stone....

Penda for deep songs like;

It's been a long time coming but change is going to come.

Drums - Mende, Spirit - Cenke

Stingy brim, freckled Nutso

Willow brook hymns, Jordan soul food

Mood of the 70s, Zulu moved through you DNA

Personification of Claude McKay – "If we must die"

If only I were so brave.

Left a black hole in my soul

May never be filled or healed

Burnt sage, nag champa

The rage refuses to go away, when they laid you in that box

Something in my spirit started to rot, like old ham hocks
On hot concrete - in July.

Struggling to breath, struggling to believe.

I close my eyes but I see you

We fought but our brotherhood was true

You were resolute in the pursuit of revolution

And I, in the evolution of peaceful solutions

You were more down to shoot, I knew that about you.

We studied the bible, Malcolm and the Panthers

Trying to heal the cancers of these inner city blues

Your face plastered all over the news.

All I could think about was why didn't I get back to you?

We had different formations

You minister of defense, me of information

Both chasing freedom

Knowing all along, you would be the first to take slugs and return some

Against tanks, dogs and guns

At dawn when the tear gas burns, the whole world would know

Surrender was never your trump card

Hard life, hard death.

The only easy is in eternity, I appreciate you visiting my dream.

And we will continue that conversation I arrive.

AKoldPiece

Haiku

They're mowing the lawn
Blades left lying in the street
Onlookers appalled

~

Taught to hate myself
Systematically place
Designed to oppress

~

KiSwahili haiku:

Papekee Penda
Rojo ajuu amenta
Kallamu Shari

Translation:
Private love
Spirit high creating heaven on earth
Penned love poem
~

Teach us to forecast
You've seen the monsoons of life
The floods never left

~

(Part 1)
Parents have no choice
They are forced to till the ground
Urban gardeners

(Part 2)
This ground ain't fertile
They keep burying seeds
Knowing they won't grow

Pam Ward

Breast Milk

Dear Dixie,
Descendant
of slave ships & chains.
The original midnight creep
creating a whole race from rape.
Hey, Slave Monger!
El Capitan of unclean!
Feasting on hatred
Maker of flesh & bone slaves
Home-Wrecker
Cracker
Mr. Burrito White Supreme!
Hey, Blood Spiller.
Yo! Petri Dish of Disease.
Breeder of sons you don't want.
Singer of anthems on greed.
Waving your red treasonous flag
like some sick badge of honor.
Segregationist!
Desecrationist!
Spawn of the burnt-cross lawn.
Heir of the German Shepherd
Papa Lynch Mob Grenade.
Descendant of nurse maids
suckling breast but taught
to detest her face.
Hey white boy!
Yeah, you!

The fool with the gun.
Killing six women and three men
claiming you're saving your race!
Listen, I know you can't blame
your idiot genes
but stop biting the titty that feeds.

Panther Mothers

sung to chant, "Oh Mary Mack." Dedicated to those murdered in church in Charleston, S.C.

Oh Mary, Mack, Mack, Mack
All dressed in black, black, black
With 25 bullets, bullets, bullets
Strapped to her back, back, back.
She went to church, church, church.
Knelt down to pray, pray, pray.
Unzipped her jacket, jacket, jacket.
Tapped her beret, ray, ray.
She channeled Huey, Huey, Huey
and H. Rap Brown, Brown, Brown.
She asked those brothers, brothers, brothers
to help her now, now, now!
She didn't want this, this, this.
But just in case, case, case
Mary was ready, ready, ready
with guns and grace, grace, grace.

Jawanza Dumisani

Nightmare

Two fish eagles lull a village
as red belly piranha
excrete the forgotten.
Lost lives forget nothing.

Like cobras through wet grass
strange ships thread Guinea's coast.
Christopher's rat-run galleon
brands *olas de sangre* into my sleep.

His rum soaked scowl
strangles a Hispaniola sun,
fan me niggar!
Hulls belch bodies,

Santa Maria's carnage swells oceans indigo,
Ferdinand never sleeps. Eulogy's drum
stretched one hundred
fifty thousand suns.

Isabella's Igbo, Asante, Dogon
gutted by countless tides.
Colonized bones writhe on beaches
old dead bury the new.

Overseers smash drums, a hush
solemn as moon glow, gag fields
from New England to Toussaint's revolt.

Me dream, watch massa' boil 'n Legba's curse.

Night stalks like a bounty. Till
spells defiance, his purpled body
leaks Tallahatchie River. Wisdom
leaps into my mouth, I count limbs
as white hoods gallop in my head.

High-strung summer of '71,
my quo vadis and five afros
tightrope the interstate
in a '63 drop-top Buick LaSabre,

hustling Jackson Five glossies, Indiana
westward, to the bayou and back,
chasing Michael from his skin
lifetimes before the bleach and burn.

Like a gauntlet of hoses
a *colored only* water fountain
outside Biloxi, cages my thirst in anger,
cop's leer crouched
south of *serve & protect.*

The Watch
(For Johanna Beer)

I

Her hand envelops mine
as if I were long lost kin.
We've barely met. Nestled
in a loveseat, a snowcapped mane
frames her easy smile,
flesh loose like a mermaid
still rose pink, radiant

as a teenage girl
the night soldiers stomp four flights
pound the door of a Vienna apartment, then disappear
into October's dark caldron with father.

II

A neighbor with empty coffins in her eyes warns,
many vanish like ghosts. Most never return.
Clinging to his fine Swiss watch
mother weeps a cello's broke string.
Quarters close in, the fifth sun surrenders.

Grandpa paces a cage of nine rooms
stalking his son's absence. Cradles the phone
like a black beacon drifting on the Wienfluss,
slumps over in a chair
long enough to exhume him, hung
in a mirror above the mantle.

Wienershnizel and challah
still warm on the stove, his neck cranes
out a half raised window below. Doubt,
diced into hope, garnishes
an untouched meal. Matzo ball simmering
wafts down a hall.

Composed as a rabbi, mother
guards the borderline of her fear,
gather everyone in the kitchen for bakashah.
Grandpa stokes the fire, stills our fears.
Clock hands grind occupation.
Fixated on his watch
time conspires against us,
ivory corpses piled in a chamber.

II

Wax hard, Sabbath broken; Yom Kippur
holiest of days, truncates into shallow sleep.
Tossed, hurried, a morsel in between.
The whole of us sways. Limboed
in a stupor; strapped to a bed
of one-eyed slumber.

Mid dawn, amid crescendos of silence
the phone rings. Only this ring blares
like a red hot siren, like squeals before slaughter.
Go ahead, answer it. A moment's journey
stretched like Exodus.

Shalom,

Shabbat shalom,
Papa!
I'm coming home.
The Seiko mother gave me
keeps better time
on Major Fleischhacker's wrist.
Elegant and faithful,
sure of its allegiance.

Derek Brown

Free-dumb!

Utter Disgrace
across proud black faces
Put there by unspeakable acts
of socially accepted degradation;
this lineage of ours
far exceeds master's cotton plantation

Back then,
We were sharecropping and working the stables,
Now we're hip hopping on major labels….
BUT AIN'T A DAMN THING CHANGED!
Cause a black man in today's society
is viewed as nothing more
than a slave with his walking papers

At the top of our lungs we're still yelling for our FREE-DOM!
Cause if you think you are truly free, then **you're** dumb

We casted votes
that were never counted
so that Obama could run the show
But if you look at the news
on any given night,
you'll see just how much further we still have to go.

Chemical trails sprayed in our air
Police brutality on the ground
Hands up or hands down

we still can't seems to breathe

This skin that I'm in
is far from the original color of sin
So someone tell me
why, oh why, oh why
It's used daily…. to paint this hell… upon me…upon we?

Slaughterhouse

Today's headlines
give my forehead lines
Stress etched into my face
from the public genocide of my race

Klansmen in white
have become boys in blue
Trading hoods for a badge
protecting them not you

They're exempt from the laws
they enforce with brute force,
while we're forcefully forced
to endure their pitchforks

The expendable darker hues
are left beaten battered and bruised
Left to die in these streets
built on our ancestors backs
From Indigenous to imported
Whether red, brown or black

This rat race ran
with slave shackles on feet
makes cheetahs born swift
easy prey like slow sheep

As the body count rises
our outlook grows ever more grim
They have yet to realize
without us… there is no them.

Kiyatana Sapp

Hoodwinked

Did the fawning of her black friends
Over her documented Bo Derek Moments
Convince her she could pull this off?

I mean, how does one
Decide to just BE Black?

How you do not recognize your privilege
In the simple and complex decision in
Choosing to feign an ethnicity
we were lynched for innately being?

I guarantee you, it is more than the qualifying shade
of manufactured skin tones in a bottle-
instead of restocking Nude beige 125
did you opt for Caramel 350
as a "let me see" tester?

Knowing our intrinsic, complex history
Just say that you've studied us,
Wearing our carefully crafted, geometric
Hairstyles just say that you admire us yet
You will never feel the pull of ancestral
DNA strands calling you to action, mindlessly
swaying to our genetic heart beat when music
infiltrates nucleic cells
nor probably ever look at sista and have
a full blown conversation

in a wink, nod and inaudible chuckle
in the span of .52 seconds.

It is not a surface question as to can you dance –
Not all of us can dance…still
There is an innate pull at our core selves
that happens even in our simplest of two steps
You've never felt the vibes of the djembe's soul beats embedded
In your hips and hands   or was that two step acquired in a hip hop
Class?

Most mother's feel for their babies,
Their only desire is to them safe from harm —
But if I crocheted your intestines with the bones of our dead would you feel
A 10th of the angst we feel daily?

We pray prayers and drape them like fine linen across prince crowns,
Carefully stitched as not to leave any spiritual loopholes our
scriptures spackle doubts
And our "I love you's" plug
Compulsive decision making leaks

"I's" are dotted and tattooed for permanence
And "T's" are embroidered to reassure us that we
Are on the right path to
Maybe –
We have no room for
Mistakes in Amerikkka

Can you even pay Black Tax?

Does privilege subconsciously creep in
to circumvent the uncomfortable or
are you balls to the wall with this thang?

Jennifer Thompson

Mother

She paved the way
A narrow path laid out
In the face of the father being erased
Lost memories
Seeking an escape
She struggles
Father disillusioned in the world
A selfish man
Does not understand family a simple but sacred plan
Searching to find himself
Much too late
Not prepared for fatherhood
Means more money to make
Shaken by this new circumstance
Yet brings life to another
Two baby girls
Failed in his position as father
Falls short to realize with children lies restriction
Won't put his dreams aside
Ignores convictions
He doesn't listen
God's divine purpose challenged by dark forces
Now divorce hits
The image of mother and father becomes distorted

Used to a familiar security now a broken home
Her childhood traumatized

She is alone
Tears linger
Her sole source of healing.
Diagnosis?
Diseased by desolation
Pain slowly dissipates
Memories fade
Life felt worthless
Suggested remedy?
No temporary relief
To God she prays
A baron land.
Possessing no life
Forsaken.
Left empty inside
Abandoned.

Mother
Survives a beautiful struggle but suffers much
Striving to provoke a mother's tender touch
It's such a hard task tragedy never forgotten
Growing up with just a mother
Forced to fill that void
Grew up fast
Tried to forget the past
Transformation at last
Good behavior not corrupted by bad company or peers
Conquered fears
Possessed but a few friends
It was all she'd need
Forced maturity allowed her to succeed
Without the presence of her Earthly father she made it
Blessed by our Heavenly Father life preserved, He saves it

Family rooted in skepticism their religion
Her decision invested in the trinity
Her mother a lonely vessel
Marries a musician, then a folk dancer — my grandfather
My mother's mother.
Tried to please her mother instead of herself
Still she's lonely
Never could comprehend the recipe of true womanhood
Blinded by the absence of her protector
Tenderness blurred
Nurturer becomes forgotten
My mother
Seeing herself in shards of a stained glass
The mirror creates a new reflection
This too shall pass
She values creation
Learns to plant a garden, sew garments, mend things broken
Chosen
She went through a battle
But Christ fought it
The lesson she learns Christ taught it
True spiritual principles
Gained the wisdom to worship our Creator, Christ our Savior
What's vital?
She learns a man's role without an image of one to raise her
Mother, my strength
No one else like her
If there was I wouldn't trade her

Doug Kearney

Alameda Street

for Deshawn, Eric, Dallas, Jerome & Lerone

We brown boys
>play
>>stick games,
>
>say
>>nicknames

like BIG D, EVIL E;
and conjure Knievel
with jigsawed dirt bikes
and sewer curbs
for asphalt launch pads.
>We all sweat
>to know flight
>for just
>a minute.

We brown boys,
>hair
>>all knaps,
>
>wear
>>ballcaps'

broken brims. Broken rims
from hungry slamdunks,
pro-ball pipe dreams
over ice cream man's
"Pop Goes the Weasel."
> We all hunt
> change from cords',
> Bermudas
> and mamas.

We brown boys—
> smack
> > talking
> slap
> > boxing—

stay bragging and bagging,
drinking summer from hoses
and water bomb barrages.
We throw rocks at garages
making no dents.
> We all just
> trying to leave
> a mark.

*Previously published in *Fear, Some*

Tar

by the roadside, rude and odd and who
is it? won't it speak when it know better to?

every wrong word caught in its dumb trap
and how dare it think it is? the hit happen

next, as if saying to dull darkness: *hey.*
here I am being here and so *hey. hey*!

HEY! and still by the roadside, stuck,
presence to absence spattered in

that black ever mess.

*Previously published in *Verse Daily, Fourteen Hills, Patter*

C. Imani Williams

Your Truth Matters: Live to Love, Release The Rest

Shhhh. They'll say to discourage you from speaking up. Stay silent and you'll be rewarded a half-ass welcome back into the family circle. They'll claim to love you. Maybe they do. It's hard to tell when the good things like love and truth are deeply hidden under narcissism and in the folds of falsehood meant to control.

But if you speak--which you should because you deserve to LIVE and reclaim life. Trust the universe to guide you.

Set Boundaries. Saying no, works. No, I won't respond to the family drum that beats irregularly with a random text, phone call, or email every four to six months. Apology still missing. It's unwise if not impossible to find the sincerity. No works, when you need to maneuver a new world one without those with whom you share blood. Stay on the path of safety and the sojourn towards inner-peace.

Forgiveness doesn't require meet-ups and shared holidays. But it is required for you to move forward. Forgive, but know your truth. Ignore the lies kept in rotation. Stand on your truth.

Live to Love those who return it in-kind. You deserve the love that doesn't gang up seeking to destroy who you are. Know your worth. Know you have the right NOT to remain silent.
###

YOU HAVE THE RIGHT NOT TO REMAIN SILENT!

The Movement for Change is happening NOW! Wake up, Become Informed and Stay Informed.
Societal ills run the gamut and WE "The People" are Tired. Being a Black Woman In America trying to breathe while fighting ongoing systemic oppression is exhausting. The cost is too high to ignore. I don't have the luxury of turning a blind eye to systemic racism and sexism. This Black Woman chooses to NOT remain silent on The Issues of the day.

64,000 U.S. Black Women gone missing since 2010. Girls Molested and Sold into Sex Trafficking. Perpetrators include women now. Unarmed Black and Brown people dying at the hands of police on the road, in driveways and living rooms. Black Women raped and dying in police custody. Black teens unlawfully detained--dead in holding cells. Unarmed Black Men die in the back of ambulances, hands up and down. Complying with laws that exterminate within laws that uphold murder.

Mental Health and Suicide Hotlines defunded. Who do we, they, you or I call when--The Rainbow is Enuf? The shaming of Mental illness leaves those trying to breathe within its clutches seeking solace outside of being fed government rhetoric and a regimented pill schedule. Can We Talk? Cannabis is a plant that can ease PTSD and anxiety that's still regarded by many as a life destroyer instead of an enhancer that eases symptoms of dis-ease. Legalize It!

Dreams lost in scams against the elderly. Poor Black Women killed by black men who won't take NO, for an answer. Young families struggle in homeless hotels trying to breathe just above suffocation, until they can figure out next steps. Single mothers with low income jobs seeking flex time for kids' medical and dental checkups. Companies refuse work-life balance. Speak Up--and you're blacklisted, remain quiet--You die inside, stifled, silenced. A worker for corporate machines. Now. Fired. Labeled a Troublemaker.

Government Lies: Poison water pollutes the system of an entire city. The elderly regularly scammed. Reverse mortgage my ass. And the babies, what about the babies?

We the People cannot give up. We must fight the system of white supremacy. Community: You, And I Matter.

Let's Turn It Around. You Have The Right NOT to Remain Silent!
###

Biographies

AKoldPiece Father, Educator, Writer, Poet, Spokenword Artist, Motivational Speaker & Host, this gentle giant has a special gift for creating haiku and short stories accented with his wit and humble personality. AKoldPiece has traveled as far as the motherland "Afraka" to share his artistry. Inspired by the legacy of his father and the future for his sun, AKP, which he is called by many, continues to embrace the unknown, where he finds solace in knowing that the unknown and uncomfortable is where true growth resides. **Khadija Anderson** (Editor) returned in 2008 to her native Los Angeles after 18 years exile in Seattle. Khadija's poetry has been published in many online and print journals. Khadija received a Pushcart Prize Nomination for her poem "Islam for Americans" and holds an MFA in Creative Writing from Antioch University Los Angeles. Her first book of poetry, *History of Butoh*, was published by Writ Large Press in 2012. **Nikki Blak** is a proud Los Angeles native and lifelong resident. She was the only poet whose likeness was depicted in a Michael Massenburg Mural in the heart of Leimert Park, as well as a piece recently commissioned for the Metro Expo. She is the author of two volumes of poetry and fiction, *GIRL* and *Five-Three and Rising*. She is the 2010 LA Grand Slam Champion, has been a member of 3 different southern California slam teams, and has gone on to compete at the annual National Poetry Slam 4 times. In the coming year, Nikki looks forward to publishing her third volume of poetry, essays, and short stories, and continuing to conduct writing workshops and perform poetry nationally. **Derek D. Brown** is a poet born and raised in Los Angeles and a graduate from Community Literature Initiative's author training program at the University of Southern California.

Currently writing his way towards his first published collection of poetry, he seeks to speak for those too embarrassed or proud to claim their truth. Derek is a member of the Still Waters Writers' Collective who regularly shares his work among peers and mentors in Leimert Park at the World Stage Performance Gallery's longstanding Anansi Writers Workshop. He has also added hosting to his resume, facilitating the open mic at Vibrations Cultural Center and Tea House as well as filling in at The World Stage. **Tommy Domino** is an LA poet that has been a member of Still Waters Writers Collective since 2012. He performs frequently around Los Angeles and has been featured at readings such as 50th Anniversary Tribute to the Watts Writers Workshop, Xpressions Poetry Month, Thursday Night Vibes, and Cerritos Library, among many others. Tommy's work has been included in several local poetry anthologies. **Jawanza Dumisani** is a PEN Fellow and recipient of a 2005 PEN Award. He was selected by Beyond Baroque as an up and coming poet in the 2003 LA Poetry Festival and was the recipient of a 2002 World State scholarship through which he studied at UCLA Extension. His first chapbook *Stoetry,* was published in2003 by FarStarFire Press, and another collection was published in 2009 through Tsehai Press. His latest book, *Black Raising Cane over Red* was published in 2014 by Glover Lane Press. Jawanza's poems appear in a number of journals in print and online. He is the former Director of Literary Programming for The World Stage in Leimert Park Village in Los Angeles. **Ashaki M. Jackson** is a social psychologist and poet. She is a Cave Canem and VONA alumna whose work appears in CURA, Pluck! and Prairie Schooner among others. She is the author of two chapter-length collections – Surveillance (Writ Large

Press) and Language Lesson (MIEL). She lives in Los Angeles. **Doug Kearney**, an L.A.-based poet, performer, librettist and teacher, Doug Kearney's writing has appeared in a number of journals and anthologies. He has been a featured performer across the country and on the radio. His libretto work has earned collaborations with a number of great artists in experimental and traditional theater and opera. Doug is a Cave Canem graduate and MFA holder from CalArts where he currently teaches African American Studies. His first full-length collection, *Fear, Some* was published by Red Hen Press, and second full-length collection of poems, *The Black Automaton*, was Catherine Wagner's National Poetry Series selection and was published by Fence Books in 2009. He also received a Whiting Writers Award in 2008. **Kiyatana Sapp** is a two-time slam poet winner and an administrative case manager from South Central Los Angeles, CA. A graduate of Antioch University, Los Angeles with a M.F.A. in Creative Writing, Kiyatana has been published in several literary magazines, inclusive of San Gabriel Valley Poetry Quarterly 67 and Enclave. Kiyatana's poetry can also be found in Sounds from the Water: Synchronized Inhales and Exhales (August 2013). **Jennifer Thompson** is a prolific spoken word artist, performer and poet. Her unique poetry style and presentation incorporates various musical instruments as well as vocal accompaniments. Her powerful message is positive and uplifting. She teaches poetry to youth for California Poets in the Schools (CPITS) and is a poet for 100 Thousands Poets for Change (100TP4C) a global movement for activism and social change. Jennifer was a special guest performer at the Globe Theater in Los Angeles for the Doo Wop Music Hall of Fame Induction

Gala. She has performed for the cities of Fontana and Pasadena and in the World Peace Choir directed by John "Sly" Wilson. **Pam Ward**, a UCLA graduate and recipient of a California Arts Council Fellow in Literature and New Letters Literary Award, Pam Ward has had her poetry published in Scream When you Burn, Grand Passion, Calyx, Catch the Fire, and the newly released, Voices from Leimert Park. Pam operates her own graphic design studio, Ward Graphics as well as runs her own publishing house, Short Dress Press. Her first novel, *Want Some, Get Some*, was published by Kensington Books, in 2007. Pam has edited five anthologies and has had short stories printed in The Best American Erotica, Men We Cherish, and Gynomite. As an artist-in-resident for the City of Los Angeles and the City of Manhattan Beach, Pam also served as a board member for Beyond Baroque Literary Arts Foundation and has worked for many community arts and social/health organizations. **C. Imani Williams** is a human rights and social justice activist. She writes to empower and give voice to those silenced through systematic oppression and white supremacy. Her work has appeared in Between the Lines, Michigan Citizen, Tucson Weekly, Harlem Times, Dope Magazine, Liberal America.org, For Harriet, and various news and popular culture blogs. She takes her grits with salt, pepper, butter, and cheese. **Conney Williams** is a Los Angeles based poet, actor and performance artist originally from Shreveport, Louisiana where he worked a radio personality. He has published two poetry collections "Leaves of Spilled Spirit from an Untamed Poet (2002/2008)" and his latest, "Blues Red Soul Falsetto (2012)." His poetry has also been published in various publications and anthologies including Voices from Leimert Park; America: At the

End of the Day; and The Drumming Between Us. He is the Artistic Director at the World Stage in Leimert Park; and is a member and current Coordinator for the Anansi Writers Workshop. He has hosted several poetry venues and been a curator for many poetry/jazz events throughout Los Angeles. He has been the Poet's Stage Coordinator for the Leimert Park Book Fair for five years.

www.ingramcontent.com/pod-product-compliance
Lightning Source LLC
Chambersburg PA
CBHW072036060426
42449CB00010BA/2298